Real-World Applications for
Algebra $\frac{1}{2}$

An Incremental Development
Third Edition

John H. Saxon, Jr.

Real-World Applications by
James Sellers

SAXON PUBLISHERS, INC.

Saxon Publishers gratefully acknowledges the contributions of the following individuals in the completion of this project:

Editorial: Brian E. Rice, Matt Maloney, R. Clint Keele, Andrew C. Kershen, Sean Douglas

Editorial Support Services: Christopher Davey, Susan Toth, Jack Day, Shelley Turner

Production: Adriana Maxwell, Brenda Lopez

Printed in the United States of America

ISBN: 1-56577-267-9

Manufacturing Code: 02S0403

Preface

Over the past several years many states have begun to test students at certain grade levels for proficiency in mathematics. These tests often include "real world" applications. While mathematics students who use Saxon materials have consistently performed well on these examinations, many of our loyal Saxon customers have expressed the desire for some additional practice in "real world" problems to prepare their students for these assessments. With that need in mind, this text has been developed to help students connect the mathematics in *Algebra $\frac{1}{2}$* to real-world situations.

This book has been written with a general goal of providing approximately one problem for every two lessons in Saxon Publishers' *Algebra $\frac{1}{2}$* textbook, for a total of sixty problems. The problems are meant to be photocopied for student use, and each page has sufficient space for students to solve the problem. Each problem contains a reference to a specific lesson and section in *Algebra $\frac{1}{2}$*. Students should refer to the section indicated when they need help with the required mathematics.

Algebra $\frac{1}{2}$ Real-World Applications should be viewed as supplementary to the *Algebra $\frac{1}{2}$* text. The problems are by no means meant to replace the ones in the text. I do not envision that all sixty problems will be used by a particular educator in one academic year. So I encourage you to peruse the problems and select those exercises that you believe would benefit students in your classroom.

acknowledgments　As I complete this project, many people deserve considerable thanks. I greatly appreciate Don Leitzle, Tony Fleury, and Mark Mutler in Shikellamy, Pennsylvania, for their guidance and insights from the classroom. I hope that they, as well as many others who teach Saxon mathematics, will be able to use this text to help students apply mathematics to their lives more easily. I am grateful to Neil Smith of Saxon Publishers for his desire and vision in seeing this project come to fruition and to Frank Wang for choosing me to complete this task. I also thank the many people at Saxon Publishers who provided technical help during this process. This includes Eric Atkins, Kelly Blass, Chris Braun, Erin Brown, Melissa Brown, Chris Davey, Stephanie Hall, Clint Keele, David LeBlanc, Brian Rice, Nancy Rimassa, Eric Scaia, Sunnie Wagner, Tanya Warren, and Loren White for their help in editing, typesetting, and graphics design. Finally, I thank my wife, Mary, for her patience and encouragement while I developed the problems and solutions contained in this book. She has always been my best supporter, and I am truly grateful for her impact on my life.

James A. Sellers, Ph.D.
Cedarville College
Cedarville, Ohio
May 2000

Implementation

Algebra $\frac{1}{2}$ is based on two key concepts: incremental development and continual review. Incremental development means that concepts are introduced in small, comprehensible increments. Continual review means that once an increment is introduced it is never dropped; rather it is practiced throughout the year. There are two plans for using these exercises. The first, Plan A, uses the exercise to help introduce the new increment taught in the lesson. The second, Plan B, uses the exercise to provide further application and review of that concept several lessons later. Each exercise indicates the lesson number where the concepts necessary to solve the problem are introduced.

Real-World Problem	Title	Concept	Use with Lesson ...	
			Plan A (To help introduce concept)	Plan B (To help apply and review concept)
1	A Trip to the Bank	Addition	1	5
2	The Air Force Recruiter	The Number Line and Ordering	2	6
3	The Family Room	Multiplication	4	8
4	From Dawn to Dusk	Addition and Subtraction Word Problems	5	9
5	The Gas Bill	Multiplying Decimal Numbers	7	11
6	New Baseboards	Perimeter	9	13
7	The Three-Way Split	Divisibility	10	14
8	Mrs. Jones's Jelly Beans	Word Problems About Equal Groups	11	15
9	Prime Parents	Prime and Composite Numbers	12	16
10	Cutting the Grass on the Football Field	Areas of Rectangles	17	22
11	Guards, Forwards, and Centers	Multiplying Fractions and Whole Numbers	18	23
12	Sibling Splitting	Multiplying Fractions	19	21
13	It's Not Rocket Science	Average	21	25
14	A Ton of Rocks	Unit Multipliers	23	27
15	I Hate Wisdom Teeth	Metric System	24	28
16	No Pressure!	Mode, Median, Mean, and Range	26	30
17	Ezequiel Alejandro, Part 1	Areas of Triangles	27	31
18	Pineapple Pizza?	Graphs	29	33
19	Farmer Brown's Bar Graph	Graphs	29	33

Real-World Problem	Title	Concept	Use with Lesson ...	
			Plan A (To help introduce concept)	**Plan B** (To help apply and review concept)
20	Tile Away	Rate	34	38
21	Survey Says!	Rectangular Coordinates	38	42
22	More Soup, Please	Division Rule	40	44
23	Reco's Score	Overall Average	41	45
24	Senior Project	Multiplying Mixed Numbers	43	47
25	Painting the Concession Stand	Multiplying Mixed Numbers	43	47
26	How Big is This Pool?	Volume	45	49
27	Can We Play?	Fractional Equations	48	52
28	Lin's Room	Surface Area	49	53
29	Go, Team!	Scientific Notation for Numbers Greater Than Ten	50	54
30	Get Rich Quick?	Percent	53	57
31	Oval Rover	Equations with Mixed Numbers	56	60
32	Out for a Sunday Drive	The Distance Problem	58	62
33	The Friendly Skies	The Distance Problem	58	65
34	Shopping at the Super Store	Solving Equations in Two Steps	61	63
35	Paving the Way, Part 1	Semicircles	64	68
36	Fertilizer Frenzy	Using Proportions with Similar Triangles	65	69
37	Any Money Left?	Rules for Addition of Signed Numbers	70	74
38	Tanks a Lot	Right Circular Cylinders	73	77
39	Fueling the Fire	Right Circular Cylinders	73	87
40	Coach's Corner	Inserting Parentheses	74	78
41	Light-Years Away	Multiplication with Scientific Notation	76	78
42	A Need for Speed?	Percents Greater Than 100	77	80
43	Flipping Veggie-Burgers	Increases in Percent	80	81

Real-World Problem	Title	Concept	Use with Lesson ...	
			Plan A (To help introduce concept)	**Plan B** (To help apply and review concept)
44	Paving the Way, Part 2	Rate Problems as Proportion Problems	83	84
45	Cable Choices	Equation of a Line	85	89
46	Sanjay and Aditi's Honeymoon	Algebraic Sentences	90	94
47	Pythagoras's Playground	Estimating Roots	92	96
48	Cycling Back?	Variables on Both Sides	95	99
49	Cheap Pizza?	Two-Step Problems	97	100
50	Popcorn Profits	Two-Step Problems	97	100
51	Scripting the Score	Advanced Ratio Problems	100	104
52	A Voluminous Earth	Multiplication of Exponential Expressions	101	105
53	Pole Position	Classifying Triangles; Angles in Triangles	104	108
54	College Close to Home	Fractional Percents	108	112
55	Compounded Currency	Compound Interest	109	113
56	How Much Are Those Cloggies in the Window?	Markup and Markdown	110	114
57	The Li Family	Probability, Part 1	112	116
58	The Jelly Bean Mystery	Probability, Part 2: Independent Events	114	118
59	Ezequiel Alejandro, Part 2	Pythagorean Theorem	117	121
60	Roofing the Pyramids?	Surface Area of Pyramids and Cones	120	123

Lesson 1: Addition

Applies in the real world to: Bank Tellers, Employees, Banking Customers

A Trip to the Bank

Your boss sends you on an errand to the bank. You are to deposit 100 one-dollar bills, 10 five-dollar bills, a roll of 40 quarters, 25 dimes, and 92 pennies. How much money should the teller say has been deposited?

Lesson 2: The Number Line and Ordering

Applies in the real world to: Air Force Recruiters, Human Resource Assistants

The Air Force Recruiter

After building a specialized fighter jet, the Air Force realized that the height of any pilot of the jet could be at most 66 inches. Consequently, the Air Force added an extra piece of data to its recruit files: the number of inches that a recruit's height differs from 66 inches. For example, if James is 72 inches tall, his file includes a 6. If John is 63 inches tall, his file includes a –3. (The negative sign indicates that his height is **below** the maximum allowable height.)

The recruiter just received files on 12 recruits. Their respective height numbers are:

    –8   10   6   4   –2   1   0   –3   5   –2   –11   3

(a) Arrange the recruits' height numbers to show shortest to tallest.

(b) How many of these recruits are eligible to fly the specialized fighter jet?

Lesson 4: Multiplication

Applies in the real world to: Building Contractors, Flooring Contractors, Homeowners

The Family Room

I have a large, square-shaped family room that measures 27 feet on a side.

(a) How many square yards does the floor of this room cover? (*Hint:* 1 yard equals 3 feet, and 1 square yard equals 9 square feet.)

(b) The carpet I like costs $7.99 per square yard. How much will it cost to buy this carpet for my family room?

(c) If installation costs an additional 22¢ per square yard, what will be my total expense for carpet and installation?

Lesson 5: Addition and Subtraction Word Problems

Applies in the real world to: Meteorologists, Farmers, Weather Enthusiasts

From Dawn to Dusk

At dawn the temperature was 42°F. By 5:00 p.m. the temperature had risen 33°F to its highest value for the day. Between 5:00 p.m. and dusk the temperature fell 12°F.

(a) What was the temperature at dusk?

(b) If a cold front passes through during the night causing the temperature to drop 32°F before dawn, what will be the temperature then?

(c) What type of warning would you expect a meteorologist to have issued the evening before?

Lesson 7: Multiplying Decimal Numbers

Applies in the real world to: Homeowners, Natural Gas Distributors

The Gas Bill

The cost of one cubic foot of natural gas in my town is $0.6035. My meter reading on July 31 was 1518. On August 31 it was 1603. The meter measures natural gas used in cubic feet.

(a) How many cubic feet of gas did I use in the month of August (between the two meter readings)?

(b) What was my total gas cost for the month? Round your answer to the nearest cent.

Lesson 9: Perimeter

Applies in the real world to: Homeowners, Carpenters, Flooring Contractors

New Baseboards

Baseboards must be installed in many rooms of a new home. (Baseboards line the perimeter of a room, covering the joint formed by the wall and the floor.) The rooms requiring baseboards have the following dimensions (in feet):

$$12 \times 12 \qquad 6 \times 8 \qquad 10 \times 12 \qquad 15 \times 10 \qquad 24 \times 10 \qquad 12 \times 11$$

(a) How many total feet of baseboard are needed?

(b) If the hardware store sells baseboard only in 9-foot sections, how many sections must be bought? (The sections can be spliced together.)

(c) How much baseboard will remain unused?

Lesson 10: Divisibility

Applies in the real world to: Business Partners

The Three-Way Split

Three friends run a car wash on the weekends. Each wash costs exactly $1, with an additional $2 charge to have the interior cleaned. They only accept payment in $1 bills (to keep the finances simple).

Over the course of the year, the three have earned a total of $721. Mo (one of the friends) thinks that the money can be split between them without needing any coins for change. Determine whether he is right **without the aid of a calculator,** and explain your answer in terms of divisibility rules.

Lesson 11: Word Problems About Equal Groups

Applies in the real world to: Teachers, Students

Mrs. Jones's Jelly Beans

Mrs. Jones has 823 jelly beans for her 55 students. She will distribute as many jelly beans as possible so that each student receives the same number of jelly beans.

(a) How many jelly beans will each student receive?

(b) If Mrs. Jones gets the extras, the ones not given to the students, how many will she have?

Lesson 12: Prime and Composite Numbers

Applies in the real world to: Parents, Children

Prime Parents

Your parents are simply crazy about mathematics, especially prime numbers. So they devised the following scheme for your allowance: They will number the weeks of the year from 1 to 52. On Week 1, they will pay you $1. On weeks that are numbered by a prime, they will pay you $3. On weeks numbered by a composite, they will pay you $5.

(a) How much money will you receive over the course of the year?

(b) Would you benefit from asking them to pay $5 on "prime weeks" and $3 on "composite weeks"?

Lesson 17: Areas of Rectangles

Applies in the real world to: Lawn Care Professionals

Cutting the Grass on the Football Field

(a) Determine the length and width of a regulation football field, including the end zones. If possible, measure an actual football field in your vicinity.

(b) Using the information in Part (a), find the area of the field.

(c) If it takes 45 seconds to cut one path across the width of the field, how long will it take to cut the whole field? (Assume the paths are cut with no overlap and that each path is 2 feet wide.)

Lesson 18: Multiplying Fractions and Whole Numbers

Applies in the real world to: Coaches, Athletes

Guards, Forwards, and Centers

The high school basketball team has 14 players, of which $\frac{2}{7}$ are guards and $\frac{1}{2}$ are forwards. The rest of the players are centers. Find the number of players in each position on the team.

Lesson 19: Multiplying Fractions

Applies in the real world to: Siblings, Friends

Sibling Splitting

Dalia and her three siblings make a pepperoni pizza and decide to split it into four equally sized sections (one for each person).

(a) Dalia finds out that her best friend is coming over, so she cuts her section in half to give her friend some. What fraction of the whole pizza does Dalia now have?

(b) Two of her siblings also have a friend coming over, so they split their (combined) two sections into three equal parts to share among the three of them. What fraction of the whole pizza does each of these siblings now have?

Lesson 21: Average

Applies in the real world to: Teachers, Students, Parents

It's Not Rocket Science

Your grade in science this year is determined by your exam average for the course. You want to get at least a B in the class, which means your exam scores must average 85 or higher. Your six exam scores are 71, 89, 85, 87, 91, and 80.

(a) Will you receive a B (or higher) in science?

(b) Your teacher has offered you (and your classmates) the option of dropping your lowest and highest exam scores and using the average of the other four to compute your grade. Will you benefit under this grading option?

Lesson 23: Unit Multipliers

Applies in the real world to: Homeowners, Landscapers

A Ton of Rocks

Recently I bought a $\frac{1}{4}$ ton of pea gravel at a cost of $19 per ton and a $\frac{1}{2}$ ton of colorful garden rocks at $75 per ton. The trailer I rented has a maximum load of 1750 pounds.

(a) How many pounds of stone did I buy?

(b) Was the trailer sufficient to haul all the stone at one time?

(c) What was my total bill, excluding tax?

Lesson 24: Metric System

Applies in the real world to: Doctors, Nurses, Patients, Dentists, Pharmacists

I Hate Wisdom Teeth

You were prescribed medication for pain after having your wisdom teeth removed. The bottle, which can hold a maximum of 50 capsules, only contains 30 capsules. Each capsule, according to the label, contains 250 milligrams of pain reliever.

If you are prescribed 2 capsules every 6 hours for a total of 8 capsules per day, how many grams of pain reliever will you take in one day?

Lesson 26: Mode, Median, Mean, and Range

Applies in the real world to: Students, Teachers

No Pressure!

Due to an excused absence, you were allowed to postpone taking yesterday's mathematics exam. Your ten classmates took the exam and earned the following scores:

72   92   80   85   67   74   98   70   89   61

(a) Determine the mean of these ten exam scores.

(b) Your teacher promised that your class can have a party on Friday if it earns an average of 80 or better on this exam. What must you score on the exam so that the class can have a party?

(c) Assuming you earn a 92 on the exam, what is the median score for the class? Is it higher or lower than the mean for the class?

Lesson 27: Areas of Triangles

Applies in the real world to: Surveyors, Property Owners, Real Estate Speculators

Ezequiel Alejandro, Part 1

Ezequiel Alejandro owns the triangular plot of land $\triangle XYZ$. $XY = 260$ yards and $ZY = 120$ yards. Ezequiel hopes to buy another triangular section, an adjacent piece of land in the shape of a right triangle. (See the figure below.) Note that $XW = 100$ yards and $ZW = 360$ yards.

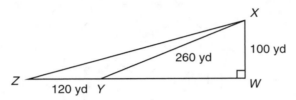

(a) Determine the area of his current plot of land.

(b) Determine the area of the plot of land Ezequiel hopes to purchase.

Lesson 29: Graphs

Applies in the real world to: Pizzeria Managers, Product Researchers

Pineapple Pizza?

Recently hundreds of people were polled at the local pizza shop to determine their favorite topping. The results of the survey were compiled in the following pie graph:

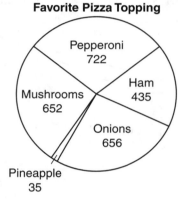

Favorite Pizza Topping

(a) How many people responded to the survey?

(b) Did the majority of those polled prefer the meat or the nonmeat toppings? Explain.

Lesson 29: Graphs

Applies in the real world to: Farmers, Agriculture Students

Farmer Brown's Bar Graph

The bar graph below illustrates the number of bushels per acre yielded by Farmer Brown's farm between 1992 and 2000.

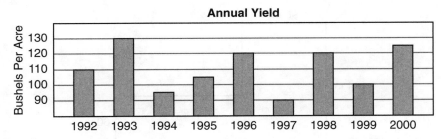

(a) From this bar graph, determine both the year in which Farmer Brown's farm had the highest yield per acre and the number of bushels per acre obtained that year.

(b) Find the median and mode for this data.

Lesson 34: Rate

Applies in the real world to: Homeowners, Flooring Contractors

Tile Away

You have been asked to help lay ceramic floor tile in a bathroom whose floor shape is shown below. (All angles are right angles.)

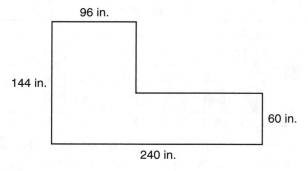

(a) Determine the area of the floor of this bathroom in square feet.

(b) Assume that a box of tiles contains 25 tiles that are 1 foot square. How many boxes of tile must you buy?

(c) How many tiles will you have left at the end of the job if you make two mistakes causing you to throw away 2 tiles?

Lesson 38: Rectangular Coordinates

Applies in the real world to: Surveyors

Survey Says!

Your boss, a surveyor, was asked recently to determine the shape of some land. He has already placed stakes at the corners of the plot of land. Relative to a landmark near the center of the land, the stakes were placed at the following locations:

> 100 feet north, 85 feet east
> 90 feet south, 70 feet east
> 95 feet north, 90 feet west
> 75 feet south, 80 feet west

(a) Using rectangular coordinates, plot the locations of the stakes, and draw the segments that form the boundary. (Assume that all boundaries are straight lines.)

(b) Is the plot of land square? Is it rectangular?

Lesson 40: Division Rule

Applies in the real world to: Engineers, Canned Goods Producers

More Soup, Please

The volume V of a cylinder with radius r and height h is $V = \pi r^2 h$.

(a) Determine the volume of a soup can with a radius of 4 cm and a height of 10 cm.

(b) Assuming the radius of a soup can must be 4 cm (for packing and shipping purposes), determine the required height of the can if it must hold 728.5 cm^3 of soup.

Lesson 41: Overall Average

Applies in the real world to: Students, Teachers, Parents

Reco's Score

Reco took 22 exams over the course of a year. During the first grading period, he took 4 exams and earned an 82 average. In the second grading period, he had 5 exams and earned an 86 average. During the third grading period, he had an average of 90 on 6 exams. During the last grading period, he earned an 85 average on the exams taken.

(a) How many exams did Reco take during the last grading period?

(b) Determine Reco's overall exam average. Round your answer to the nearest hundredth.

Lesson 43: Multiplying Mixed Numbers

Applies in the real world to: Students, Carpenters

Senior Project

For a graduation project at school, my friends and I have decided to build new dugouts for the softball field. The lumber store has offered to donate the lumber, but first we must determine how much to use. The only difficult calculation is for the eaves. We need 13 pieces that are each $2\frac{3}{4}$ feet long and that cannot be spliced together. The lumber comes in 8-foot, 10-foot, and 12-foot sections, but we can only get one length of board. Which length of board should we choose in order to minimize waste?

Lesson 43: Multiplying Mixed Numbers

Applies in the real world to: Painters

Painting the Concession Stand

You have to paint the concession stand for your local ball team. The back and side walls (both inside and outside) need painting, and the same paint can be used for both.

The two side walls measure $8\frac{3}{4}$ by $8\frac{1}{2}$ feet each, while the back wall, which is quite long, measures $12\frac{1}{3}$ yards by $8\frac{1}{2}$ feet.

(a) Determine the total area that must be painted (in square feet).

(b) Assuming that one gallon of paint will cover 250 square feet in one coat, determine the number of gallons you must buy to paint the walls with two coats.

Lesson 45: Volume

Applies in the real world to: Swimming Pool Supervisors, Engineers

How Big is This Pool?

A local swimming pool is in the shape of a rectangle and measures 100 feet by 75 feet. The floor of the pool gently slopes from each end to the center, going from a depth of $2\frac{1}{2}$ feet (for the kids) to a depth of 8 feet. See the diagram below.

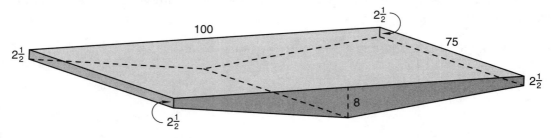

(a) Determine the volume of this pool in cubic feet. (It might help to turn the pool "on its side.")

(b) If 20 cubic feet of water can be pumped into the pool per minute, approximately how many hours will it take to fill the pool?

Lesson 48: Fractional Equations

Applies in the real world to: Coaches, Student Athletes, Booster Club Members, Parents, Equipment Managers

Can We Play?

The district championship game will be played on an artificial surface. Four-fifths of the team needs new shoes for the game. There are 40 players on the team, and each pair of shoes sells for $35. How much money must the booster club raise to cover the entire cost of the shoes?

Lesson 49: Surface Area

Applies in the real world to: Homeowners, Painters

Lin's Room

The walls and ceiling in one of the rooms of Lin's house need to be repainted. The floor of the room is rectangular, 20 feet by 15 feet, and has a ceiling that is 10 feet high. The doorway into the room is 3 feet by 7 feet. There are also two rectangular windows that measure 3 feet by 4 feet each. On one wall there is an 8-foot-by-7-foot closet opening.

How many feet of wall surface should Lin count on painting?

Lesson 50: Scientific Notation for Numbers Greater Than Ten

Applies in the real world to: Purchasing Agents

Go, Team!

The local university football stadium seats 60,000 fans, and the average attendance at home games is 48,500. It has been determined that an average fan consumes 2.25 soft drinks per game.

(a) Determine the total number of cups used during an average game. Express your answer in scientific notation.

(b) Next week is the homecoming game, which is always sold out. You need to order cups, and you know each box contains 1×10^3 cups. How many boxes should you order?

Lesson 53: Percent

Applies in the real world to: Workers

Get Rich Quick?

You just got your first job, and you are extremely excited about getting rich! You make $6.25 per hour, and you work 25 hours per week.

(a) Before any taxes or other deductions are taken from your check, how much money will you earn in a week? (This is called your **gross weekly income.**)

(b) You have learned that, for taxes, insurance, and all other deductions, 24% of your earnings will be taken, and you will be paid the rest. How much money will you take home in a week? (This is called your **net weekly income.**)

(c) Your parents require that you save 10% of your net earnings each week. How much savings will you accumulate in one year (52 weeks)?

Lesson 56: Equations with Mixed Numbers

Applies in the real world to: Walkers, Health Enthusiasts, Trainers

Oval Rover

You want to walk around an oval track 40 times in one hour, and you notice that you can complete one lap in $2\frac{1}{2}$ minutes with no difficulty.

(a) How many laps can you complete in one hour at this pace?

(b) How long will it take you to complete your goal of 40 laps?

Lesson 58: The Distance Problem

Applies in the real world to: Travelers, Motorists

Out for a Sunday Drive

My cousin in Philadelphia recently invited me to a basketball game. The game starts at 7:30, and I told him I would pick him up an hour before the game. The game is on the weekend, so I know I will encounter some slow traffic on the way. For the first 75 miles of the trip, I will only average about 40 mph. (The route goes through various small towns and traffic lights.) For the last 100 miles, I will be on a major highway and will average 65 mph. Assuming that I stop 20 minutes for a burger and fries and another 10 minutes at a rest area, determine what time I must leave my home for this trip (to the nearest minute).

Lesson 58: The Distance Problem

Applies in the real world to: Pilots, Air Traffic Controllers

The Friendly Skies

One morning I flew from Dayton, Ohio, to St. Louis, Missouri, a distance of 334 miles. I left Dayton at 6:15 a.m. local time and arrived in St. Louis at 6:45 a.m. local time. That afternoon, I flew out of St. Louis at 4:00 p.m. local time and arrived in Pittsburgh, Pennsylvania, at 7:00 p.m. local time. The distance from St. Louis to Pittsburgh is about 562 miles. (*Note:* St. Louis is in a different time zone from Dayton and Pittsburgh.)

Determine the average speed of each plane in miles per hour.

Lesson 61: Solving Equations in Two Steps

Applies in the real world to: Consumers

Shopping at the Super Store

Yesterday I went to my local Super Store. I bought a new paint roller and roller pan for $6.97, a gallon of milk for $1.99, a magazine for $1.19, and two identical gallons of paint without marked prices. Ignoring tax, I paid a total of $40.53.

(a) Set up an equation that describes this situation, letting x be the price of one gallon of paint.

(b) Find the price for each gallon of paint.

Lesson 64: Semicircles

Applies in the real world to: Homeowners, Contractors

Paving the Way, Part 1

A new homeowner wants to build a semicircular driveway, as shown in the diagram below.

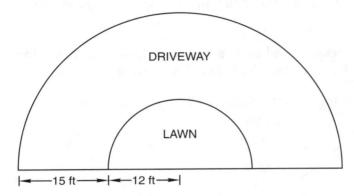

The driveway must be 6 inches thick. Determine the number of cubic yards of paving material needed to complete this job.

Lesson 65: Using Proportions with Similar Triangles

Applies in the real world to: Farmers, Surveyors

Fertilizer Frenzy

A local farmer wishes to fertilize one of his fields, but he must first find its area. The field is in the shape of the triangle shown below. After making some measurements, the farmer knows the following information:

> Line *A* is 18 feet long and parallel to side *B*. Line *A* is 15 feet from the apex of the triangle. The total length of side *C* is 900 feet.

What is the total area of the field in square feet?

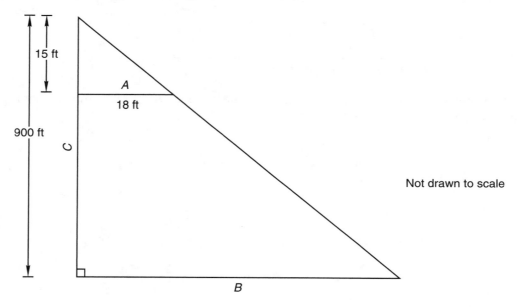

Lesson 70: Rules for Addition of Signed Numbers

Applies in the real world to: Checking Account Holders

Any Money Left?

You open a checking account on the first day of the month with $500. Every day for the next fourteen days, you withdraw $30. On the fifteenth day you deposit two checks, each worth $712. Over the next three days you make three withdrawals that total $65. After these three withdrawals, what is your balance?

Lesson 73: Right Circular Cylinders

Applies in the real world to: City Planners, Painters

Tanks a Lot

A local town wants to paint the entire exposed surface of its water tank. The tank is in the shape of a cylinder. Because it is elevated, the bottom surface needs to be painted. The diameter of the tank is 30 feet and the height is 20 feet. Paint costs $22 per gallon and is only sold in whole gallons. Only one coat is necessary to paint the tank. If one gallon covers approximately 250 square feet, how many full gallons of paint should the town purchase?

Lesson 73: Right Circular Cylinders

Applies in the real world to: Petroleum Facility Managers, Engineers, Plant Supervisors

Fueling the Fire

Your job at a fuel plant is to make sure there are enough holding tanks for the heating oil waiting to be shipped. Your cylindrical fuel tanks are 85 feet tall, each with a diameter of 32 feet. One million cubic feet of oil is being shipped to your plant for storage. How many fuel tanks will you need?

Lesson 74: Inserting Parentheses

Applies in the real world to: Coaches, Football Players, Sports Fans

Coach's Corner

Our football coach has been analyzing each drive by the football team's offense to see whether it is consistently keeping the ball for a good amount of time before the defense must retake the field. During the first drive of last week's game, which began on our own 20-yard line, he noted the following:

Play 1: Gained 6 yards

Play 2: Lost 2 yards

Play 3: Gained 9 yards

Play 4: Gained 8 yards

Play 5: Lost 9 yards

Play 6: Gained 18 yards

Play 7: Gained 12 yards

Play 8: Interception thrown (defense retakes the field)

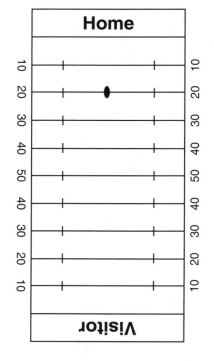

(a) How many first downs did the offense earn before the drive ended? (To earn a first down, a team must advance a total of 10 yards from the spot of the previous first down in four or fewer consecutive plays.)

(b) At what yard line was the team before Play 8 took place?

Lesson 76: Multiplication with Scientific Notation

Applies in the real world to: Astronomers

Light-Years Away

It is well known to scientists that the speed of light in a vacuum is approximately 186,000 miles per second. For expressing distances from the earth to stars and other objects far away, scientists use a unit of measurement known as the light-year. A light-year is the distance light can travel in one year.

(a) Express the speed of light (in miles per second) in scientific notation.

(b) Determine the number of seconds in one year (365 days). Express this result in scientific notation.

(c) Using Parts (a) and (b), determine the speed of light in miles per year.

(d) Proxima Centauri, the star nearest to the Sun, is about 4.2 light-years away. Estimate the distance to Proxima Centauri in miles. Express your answer in scientific notation.

Lesson 77: Percents Greater Than 100

Applies in the real world to: Car Owners, Insurance Agents

A Need for Speed?

You were recently given a speeding ticket, which meant that your parents' monthly insurance premium increased. Before the ticket, their insurance cost $176 per month. It now costs $207 per month.

(a) What percent of $176 is $207?

(b) Translate your answer from Part (a) into a statement about the percentage increase charged by your parents' insurance company.

(c) Your parents have decided to make you pay for the increase in their monthly insurance premium. How much money will you owe your parents for a year's worth of insurance payments?

Lesson 80: Increases in Percent

Applies in the real world to: Hourly Employees

Flipping Veggie-Burgers

Over the past three years, you have been an excellent employee at a local vegetarian restaurant. When you started your job, you made $5.75 per hour. At your three annual reviews (one at the end of each year), your hourly wage has increased to $6.00, $6.40, and $7.00, respectively.

(a) Determine the percent increase of each wage change. (You must calculate three separate percentage increases.)

(b) Calculate the percentage increase between $5.75 and $7.00 (your original hourly wage and your current hourly wage).

(c) Do the percentages in Part (a) sum to the percentage found in Part (b)? Is this a problem?

Lesson 83: Rate Problems as Proportion Problems

Applies in the real world to: Homeowners, Contractors

Paving the Way, Part 2

In Problem 35 we encountered a homeowner who was building a semicircular driveway 6 inches deep. The homeowner is having trouble choosing a paving material. Concrete sells for $75.40 per cubic yard. Asphalt costs $29.70 per ton, and a cubic yard of asphalt weighs 1.5 tons.

(a) Determine the cost of paving the driveway with each of the materials mentioned above. (*Note:* You should have calculated the volume of the driveway in Problem 35 to be 17.02 cubic yards.)

(b) Which material is less expensive for the job and by how much?

Lesson 85: Equation of a Line

Applies in the real world to: Cable Subscribers, Cable Providers

Cable Choices

Two competing cable companies offer different basic viewing plans. Company 1 costs $80 for installation and $24 per month. Company 2 costs $120 for installation and $16 per month. The equations below give the cost in dollars (y) of subscribing to each of the cable companies for x months.

$$\text{Company 1: } y = 24x + 80$$
$$\text{Company 2: } y = 16x + 120$$

(a) Graph the two cost equations on a single coordinate plane.

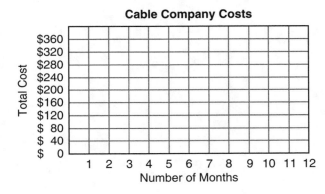

(b) After how many months of service will the total cost be the same for both companies?

(c) If you will have cable for only three months, which company offers the better deal?

(d) If you will subscribe for more than eight months, which company offers the better deal?

Lesson 90: Algebraic Sentences

Applies in the real world to: Newlyweds, Bicyclists, Bicycle Shop Owners

Sanjay and Aditi's Honeymoon

While on their honeymoon, Sanjay and Aditi decide to spend an afternoon biking. They will need to rent the bikes, and there are two companies in town to choose from. Beau's Bikes charges $10 per hour per bike. Celine's Cycles charges only $4 per hour per bike, but with an initial fixed fee of $15 per bike.

Let t represent the time one bike is rented (in hours) and y represent the total cost of renting one bike. Write algebraic sentences for the two bike shops that describe the cost of renting a bike for t hours.

Lesson 92: Estimating Roots

Applies in the real world to: City Planners, Purchasing Agents

Pythagoras's Playground

The local playground has a very large sandbox in the shape of a right triangle. As noted in the figure below, the lengths of the two short sides (the legs) are 5 yards and 9 yards, respectively.

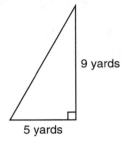

9 yards

5 yards

By the Pythagorean theorem, the length of the longest side (the hypotenuse) is $\sqrt{106}$ yards.

(a) Estimate the length of the hypotenuse by determining the two consecutive integers between which $\sqrt{106}$ is bounded.

(b) The city has decided to replace the rotting and splintering wood that forms the longest side. The type of wood to be used only comes in 12-foot lengths. How many pieces of wood should the city purchase?

(c) About how much wood will remain unused when the construction job is finished?

Lesson 95: Variables on Both Sides

Applies in the real world to: Newlyweds, Bicycle Shop Owners

Cycling Back?

We return again to those love-stricken newlyweds from Problem 46, Sanjay and Aditi. We represented the cost of renting a bike for t hours at each shop with an algebraic sentence. At Beau's Bikes the cost was $y = 10t$. At Celine's Cycles it was $y = 4t + 15$.

(a) Sanjay and Aditi are now trying to determine the amount of time t at which the cost of renting a bike is the same for both companies. Help them by determining this amount of time.

(b) If they plan to rent for only two hours, which company should they choose?

Lesson 97: Two-Step Problems

Applies in the real world to: Friends, Caterers, Hosts

Cheap Pizza?

You are planning to have 20 friends over for a party this weekend. To reduce costs, each friend has pitched in $1, and you plan to make cheese pizzas to eat. You have calculated that for each pizza the cheese will cost 75¢, the tomato sauce will cost 40¢, and the ingredients for the crust will cost 60¢.

(a) How much will the ingredients for each pizza cost?

(b) How many whole pizzas can you make with the money donated by your friends?

(c) How many whole pizzas can you make if you pay $1 as well?

Lesson 97: Two-Step Problems

Applies in the real world to: Concessions Managers

Popcorn Profits

After collecting tickets for three years, you are finally promoted to weekend manager of the local movie theater. You want to do well at your new job, so you try to increase profits.

The cost for a bucket of popcorn is as follows: the popcorn kernels and butter used in each bucket cost 5¢ and 2¢, and the bucket itself costs a quarter. Each bucket of popcorn sells for $3.00.

(a) In one night you sold 115 buckets. What was your profit?

(b) You really want to please your boss, so you decide to increase profits by charging more per bucket. How much must you charge for a bucket of popcorn to make a $365.70 profit from selling 115 buckets?

Lesson 100: Advanced Ratio Problems

Applies in the real world to: Coaches, Athletes, Sports Reporters

Scripting the Score

The top three scorers on the basketball team scored a total of 1216 points this season in the ratio of 5 to 2 to 1.

(a) How many points did each player score during the season?

(b) The third-highest scorer scored what percentage of the highest scorer's total?

Lesson 101: Multiplication of Exponential Expressions

Applies in the real world to: Geologists, Physicists

A Voluminous Earth

Many scientists have worked very hard to determine the diameter of the earth. It has been found to be approximately 1.275×10^7 meters.

It is also known that the volume V of any sphere is given by $V = \frac{4}{3}\pi r^3$, where r is the radius of the sphere. Assuming our planet is a sphere, calculate its volume.

Lesson 104: Classifying Triangles; Angles in Triangles

Applies in the real world to: Telephone and Electric
Company Workers

Pole Position

Two wooden telephone poles stand vertically with their bases 80 feet apart on a level street. One
of the poles stands 50 feet high; the other, 40 feet high. Each pole has a stabilizing wire attached to
the top of the pole and stretched to a common anchor point on the ground exactly halfway between
the bases of the two poles.

(a) Classify by sides and by angles the triangle made by the 40-foot pole, its stabilizing wire, and
the ground.

(b) Assume the angle made by the 50-foot pole and its stabilizing wire is 39°. Determine the
angle made by the ground and this wire.

(c) If a telephone wire is strung tightly between the tops of the two poles, what can be said about
the triangle made by the three wires?

Lesson 108: Fractional Percents

Applies in the real world to: Students, Teachers, School Counselors, School Administrators, Scholarship Sponsors

College Close to Home

There are 350 people in our graduating class, of which 200 are boys. National averages indicate that $23\frac{1}{2}\%$ of all male high school graduates and $19\frac{2}{3}\%$ of all female high school graduates attend college within 175 miles of their high schools. Assuming our graduating class conforms to national averages, how many students in our class will attend college within 175 miles of our high school?

Lesson 109: Compound Interest

Applies in the real world to: Investors

Compounded Currency

You want to save money to buy a $2000 car. Currently, you have $1000, which you earned from your job. A local bank offers a quarterly interest rate of 1% compounded quarterly on its savings accounts.

(a) Determine the balance in such an account after two years, assuming a $1000 initial deposit and no additional deposits or withdrawals.

(b) Given that you want to buy the car within two years, what does Part (a) imply about the bank's savings plan?

Lesson 110: Markup and Markdown

Applies in the real world to: Thrifty Shoppers

How Much Are Those Cloggies in the Window?

Stephanie goes shopping during a storewide sale where everything is marked down. She finds two pairs of clogs on the shelf labeled "$\frac{1}{3}$ off" and three shirts marked "$\frac{2}{5}$ off." The clogs normally sell for $33.99 per pair, and the shirts usually sell for $18.00 each.

Stephanie would like to buy all five items, but she has just $70 in cash. Assuming no sales tax on clothing items, does she have enough to pay the full amount in cash? If so, how much money will she have left over? If she does not have enough money to pay the whole amount, how much more money will Stephanie need?

Lesson 112: Probability, Part 1

Applies in the real world to: Genealogists

The Li Family

The Li family has four children born in different years.

(a) List all possible arrangements of boy and girl children that the Li family could have.

(b) Using the answer to Part (a), find the probability that the Li family has exactly two boys and two girls in some order.

Lesson 114: Probability, Part 2: Independent Events

Applies in the real world to: Candy Fanatics

The Jelly Bean Mystery

According to the friendly people at the local candy store, the ratio of colors of jelly beans is not chosen randomly. There is a color ratio to which the manufacturers adhere when they make the candies. The number of jelly beans of each color in a bag of 100 is as follows: 20 each of yellow, red, brown, and blue, and 10 each of green and orange.

(a) In a random blind selection, what is the probability of picking a green jelly bean first and a red one second?

(b) In a new bag of 100 jelly beans, what is the probability of picking an orange jelly bean followed by another orange jelly bean, both at random?

Lesson 117: Pythagorean Theorem

Applies in the real world to: Property Owners, Real Estate Speculators, Surveyors

Ezequiel Alejandro, Part 2

Ezequiel Alejandro owns the triangular plot of land $\triangle XYZ$. He hopes to buy the adjacent plot $\triangle WXY$. Use the depiction of these two plots shown below to answer the following questions:

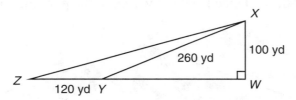

(a) Find the lengths of the two segments that are currently unknown **by using the Pythagorean theorem.**

(b) Once Ezequiel buys all of this land, he will want to fence the outer perimeter uniformly with a white, wooden fence (so it will look nice). If the wooden fence costs $8 per linear foot, how much will it cost for Ezequiel to fence in this land?

Lesson 120: Surface Area of Pyramids and Cones

Applies in the real world to: Homeowners, Roofing Contractors, Construction Workers

Roofing the Pyramids?

As a roofing contractor, you are called about a job. A building has been built that has a square base measuring 50 feet on each side. The building has a pyramid-shaped roof that needs to be shingled. You have determined that the distance from the vertex of the pyramid to the lower edge of the roof is 28 feet.

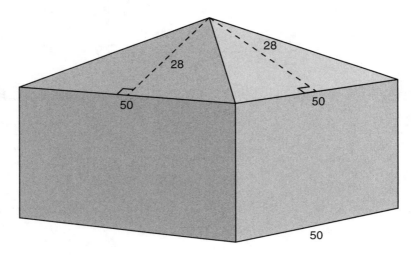

(a) How many square feet of roof needs to be shingled?

(b) If each bundle of shingles contains 20 shingles and each shingle covers 1.5 square feet, how many bundles of shingles are needed to cover the roof, assuming no waste?

Solutions

for Algebra $\frac{1}{2}$ Real-World Applications

1. The 100 one-dollar bills and 10 five-dollar bills total $150. The roll of 40 quarters increases the total by $10 to $160. The 25 dimes add $2.50 to increase the total to $162.50. Adding $0.92 from the pennies yields a total deposit of **$163.42.**

2. (a) **–11, –8, –3, –2, –2, 0, 1, 3, 4, 5, 6, 10**
   (b) **Six recruits** are eligible, including the recruit who corresponds to the number 0.

3. (a) The room measures 27 feet, or 9 yards, on a side. So the floor of the room covers 9 yards × 9 yards, or **81 square yards.**
   (b) 81 × $7.99 = **$647.19**
   (c) 81 × ($7.99 + $0.22) = **$665.01**

4. (a) The temperature at dusk was 42°F + 33°F – 12°F = **63°F.**
   (b) The temperature before dawn will be 63°F – 32°F = **31°F.**
   (c) With the temperature falling below 32°F, a good meteorologist would have issued a **freeze warning.**

5. (a) The number of cubic feet of gas used was 1603 – 1518 = **85 cubic feet.**
   (b) The cost is found by multiplying 85 by $0.6035, which yields $51.2975. Rounded to the nearest cent, this is **$51.30.**

6. (a) To find the number of feet of baseboard needed, we calculate the perimeter of each room, as shown below.

Room Dimensions	Expression of Perimeter	Value of Perimeter
12 × 12	12 + 12 + 12 + 12	48 feet
6 × 8	6 + 8 + 6 + 8	28 feet
10 × 12	10 + 12 + 10 + 12	44 feet
15 × 10	15 + 10 + 15 + 10	50 feet
24 × 10	24 + 10 + 24 + 10	68 feet
12 × 11	12 + 11 + 12 + 11	46 feet

   The total number of feet of baseboard needed is the sum of these perimeters, which is **284 feet.**
   (b) Since 284 ÷ 9 ≈ 31.55, **32 sections must be purchased.**
   (c) Thirty-two 9-foot sections is 288 feet of baseboard (found by multiplying 32 and 9). So we will have 288 – 284 = **4 feet of board left over.**

7. The problem asks whether $721 is evenly divisible by the number 3. From divisibility rules, we know that if 721 were divisible by 3, 7 + 2 + 1 must also be divisible by 3. But 7 + 2 + 1 = 10, and 10 is not evenly divisible by 3. Therefore, **Mo is not correct.**

8. (a) If we divide 823 by 55, we get approximately 14.9636. So each student will receive **14 jelly beans.**
   (b) The total number of jelly beans given to the 55 students is the product of 55 and 14, which is 770. So Mrs. Jones will receive 823 – 770, or **53 jelly beans.**

9. (a) There are 15 prime numbers from 1 to 52 (2, 3, 5, 7, 11, 13, 17, 19, 23, 29, 31, 37, 41, 43, 47). There are also 36 composite numbers. So you will receive $1 for the first week, plus $3 × 15 (for the prime weeks), plus $5 × 36 (for the composite weeks). Your total will be **$226.**

   (b) If you switch, you will make $1, plus $5 × 15, plus $3 × 36, for a total of $184. So **you would not benefit from asking them to switch.**

10. (a) Including the end zones, a football field is **120 yards long** and **160 feet wide.**

   (b) Area is length times width. The field's length is 360 feet, and its width is 160 feet, so its area is **57,600 square feet.**

   (c) If each path is 2 feet wide, then 180 paths will have to be cut across the width of the field (360 ÷ 2 = 180). The total time it will take to cut the field is 180 × 45 seconds, which is 8100 seconds. This equals 135 minutes, or **2 hours 15 minutes.**

11. There are $14 \times \frac{2}{7} = $ **4 guards.** Similarly, there are $14 \times \frac{1}{2} = $ **7 forwards.** This accounts for 11 of the 14 players, so there are **3 centers.**

12. (a) Dalia started with $\frac{1}{4}$ of the whole pizza, which she split in half to share with her friend.

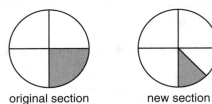

   original section   new section

   Dalia now has $\frac{1}{2} \cdot \frac{1}{4}$, or $\frac{1}{8}$ **of the whole pizza.**

   (b) Her two siblings started with $\frac{1}{4} + \frac{1}{4}$, or $\frac{1}{2}$ of the whole pizza, which they split three ways.

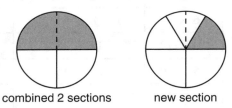

   combined 2 sections   new section

   Now each of these siblings (and their friend) has $\frac{1}{3} \cdot \frac{1}{2}$, or $\frac{1}{6}$ **of the whole pizza.**

13. (a) The average of 71, 89, 85, 87, 91, and 80 is approximately 83.83. So **you will not receive a B in science.**

   (b) Now only the scores 89, 85, 87, and 80 are used to compute your average, which is 85.25. Under this grading option, **you will receive a B in the class, which is a benefit to you.**

14. (a) A ton is 2000 pounds. I purchased $(\frac{1}{4})(2000) = 500$ pounds of pea gravel and $(\frac{1}{2})(2000) = 1000$ pounds of garden rocks, which is a total of **1500 pounds.**

   (b) **Yes,** the trailer was sufficient to haul all the stone at one time.

   (c) The bill was calculated by multiplying $19 by $\frac{1}{4}$ and $75 by $\frac{1}{2}$. That means I paid $4.75 for the pea gravel and $37.50 for the garden stones, for a total bill of **$42.25.**

15. In one day you will take 8 × 250 milligrams, which is a total of 2000 milligrams. This is equivalent to **2 grams.**

16. First we list the scores from lowest to highest:

$$61 \quad 67 \quad 70 \quad 72 \quad 74 \quad 80 \quad 85 \quad 89 \quad 92 \quad 98$$

(a) The mean is $(61 + 67 + 70 + 72 + 74 + 80 + 85 + 89 + 92 + 98) \div 10 =$ **78.8.**

(b) To find the score necessary to raise the class average to 80, we solve for x in

$$(61 + 67 + 70 + 72 + 74 + 80 + 85 + 89 + 92 + 98 + x) \div 11 = 80$$

This equation means that $788 + x = 880$. Since $x = 92$, you must score a **92** to raise the class average to 80.

(c) If you earn a 92, then the median becomes the sixth score in the list (after yours is inserted). That score would be 80 and is exactly **the same as the mean,** which was specified in Part (b).

17. (a) The triangle that forms his current plot of land has a base of 120 yards and a height of 100 yards. Therefore, the area is $\frac{1}{2} \times 120 \times 100$, or **6000 square yards.**

(b) Since $ZW = 360$ yards, $YW = 360 - 120 = 240$ yards. So the area of the new plot is $\frac{1}{2} \times 240 \times 100$, or **12,000 square yards.**

18. (a) The number of people who responded is the sum of 722, 435, 656, 35, and 652, which is **2500 people.**

(b) The meat toppings—pepperoni and ham—were preferred by $722 + 435$, or 1157 people. The other toppings were preferred by $652 + 35 + 656$, or 1343 people. So **the majority of those polled preferred the nonmeat toppings.**

19. (a) In **1993** Farmer Brown obtained **130 bushels per acre.**

(b) We first list the graph values from lowest to highest:

$$90 \quad 95 \quad 100 \quad 105 \quad 110 \quad 120 \quad 120 \quad 125 \quad 130$$

We then see that the median is **110 bushels per acre** and the mode is **120 bushels per acre.**

20. (a) The L-shaped figure can be broken into two rectangles, one that is 96 inches by 84 inches (the "top" of the L), and another rectangle that is 240 inches by 60 inches. The two rectangles have areas of 8064 and 14,400 square inches. So the area of the floor is $8064 + 14,400$, or 22,464 square inches. To convert to square feet, we divide by $12 \times 12 = 144$, since there are 12 inches in 1 foot. This yields an area of **156 square feet.**

(b) **Seven boxes of tile are needed,** since six boxes will cover only 150 square feet. (Seven boxes will cover 175 square feet.)

(c) At the end of the job, $175 - 156 - 2 =$ **17 tiles** will remain.

21. (a)

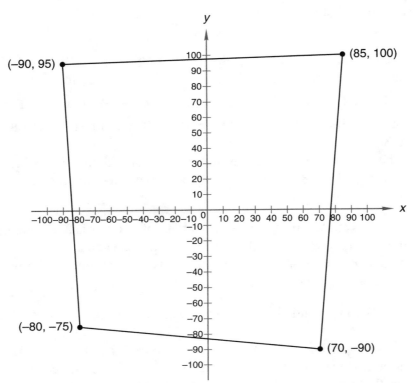

(b) From the graph in Part (a), we see that **the plot of land is neither square nor rectangular.**

22. (a) Using the formula given and 3.14 for π, we have $3.14 \times 4^2 \times 10 = $ **502.4 cm³.**
  (b) From the information given, we can write $(3.14 \times 4^2)h = 728.5$, which simplifies to $50.24h = 728.5$. Dividing both sides of this equation by 50.24 yields $h = $ **14.5 cm.**

23. (a) Reco took a total of 22 tests, so the number he took in the last grading period was $22 - 4 - 5 - 6$, or **7 exams.**
  (b) His overall average is found by dividing $[(82 \times 4) + (86 \times 5) + (90 \times 6) + (85 \times 7)]$ by the total number of exams, which is 22. Rounding to the nearest hundredth yields **86.05.**

24. Each 8-foot section could yield 2 of the $2\frac{3}{4}$-foot pieces, leaving $2\frac{1}{2}$ feet of waste. So 6 such sections would yield 12 of the $2\frac{3}{4}$-foot pieces and leave 15 feet of waste. The last $2\frac{3}{4}$-foot piece would come from a seventh board, leaving $5\frac{1}{4}$ feet of waste, for a total of $20\frac{1}{4}$ feet of waste.

Each 10-foot section could yield 3 of the $2\frac{3}{4}$-foot pieces, meaning that we would need 5 such sections. There would be $14\frac{1}{4}$ feet of waste.

Each 12-foot section could yield 4 of the $2\frac{3}{4}$-foot pieces, meaning that we would need 4 such sections. The total waste would be $12\frac{1}{4}$ feet. Therefore, we should use the **12-foot sections.**

25. (a) The exterior area of one side wall is $8\frac{1}{2} \times 8\frac{3}{4}$, or $74\frac{3}{8}$ square feet. Since there are two such walls, we double this amount to yield $148\frac{3}{4}$ square feet. Now for the back wall: Converting units to feet, we obtain the dimensions 37 feet by $8\frac{1}{2}$ feet. So the exterior area of this wall is $314\frac{1}{2}$ square feet. Hence, the exterior walls have a total area of $148\frac{3}{4} + 314\frac{1}{2}$, or $463\frac{1}{4}$ square feet. Since the exterior area is equal to the interior area, we multiply by 2 to obtain the final answer, which is **$926\frac{1}{2}$ square feet.**

(b) Painting the stand with two coats means covering 1853 square feet (double the total area of $926\frac{1}{2}$ square feet). You will require **8 gallons** of paint, which will cover 8×250, or 2000 square feet.

26. (a) If the pool is turned "on its side," the base of this figure can be thought of as a rectangle that measures 100 feet by $2\frac{1}{2}$ feet and a triangle whose base is 100 feet and whose height is $5\frac{1}{2}$ feet. Thus the area of the rectangle is $100 \times 2\frac{1}{2} = 250$ square feet, and the area of the triangle is $\frac{1}{2} \times 100 \times 5\frac{1}{2} = 275$ square feet. So the base of this figure has an area of 525 square feet. The volume is found by multiplying this area by the "height," which is 75 feet. Hence, the volume is **39,375 cubic feet.**

    (b) Divide the volume by 20 to determine the number of minutes needed to fill the pool: 1968.75. Then divide by 60 to obtain the number of hours needed to fill the pool (since there are 60 minutes in 1 hour). This yields **32.8125 hours.**

27. First multiply the number of players on the team by the fraction needing new shoes: $40 \times \frac{4}{5} = 32$. The total cost of buying new shoes for these players is $32 \times \$35$, or **\$1120.**

28. First determine the area of the walls and ceiling, ignoring the openings: The ceiling is 20 feet by 15 feet (equal to the floor dimensions), so its area is 300 square feet. Two of the walls are 20 feet by 10 feet, for a combined area of 400 square feet $[2 \times (20 \times 10)]$. The other two walls account for a combined 300 square feet. All these figures total 1000 square feet. Then subtract the area of the openings: The doorway accounts for 21 square feet, and the combined areas of the two windows is 24 square feet. The closet opening is 56 square feet. Thus, the room has $1000 - 21 - 24 - 56$, or **899 square feet** of wall and ceiling to be painted.

29. (a) Multiply 2.25 cups per fan by 48,500 fans (an average crowd) to get 109,125 cups. Expressed in scientific notation, an average of **1.09125×10^5 cups** are used.

    (b) We predict that 60,000 fans will attend, meaning that 135,000, or 1.35×10^5 cups will be used. Dividing by 1×10^3, we see that **135 boxes** are needed for homecoming.

30. (a) Your gross weekly income is simply 6.25×25, which yields a total of **\$156.25.**

    (b) The amount of money subtracted from your check is 156.25×0.24, or \$37.50. Once this is subtracted, your net weekly income is **\$118.75.**

    (c) Ten percent of one week's net income is \$11.88 (rounding up to the nearest cent). Thus, in one year (52 weeks), you will save 11.88×52, or **\$617.76.**

31. (a) One hour equals 60 minutes, so you can complete $60 \div 2\frac{1}{2}$, or **24 laps.**

    (b) Forty laps at the pace of one lap every $2\frac{1}{2}$ minutes will take $40 \times 2\frac{1}{2} = 100$ minutes, or **1 hour 40 minutes.**

32. The first 75 miles of the trip will take 1.875 hours (found by dividing 75 by 40). The remaining 100 miles of the trip will take approximately 1.538 hours (found by dividing 100 by 65). Therefore, the driving alone will take approximately 3.415 hours. Adding half an hour for dinner and the rest stop yields a total of 3.915 hours of travel (approximately 3 hours 55 minutes). Since I must pick up my cousin at 6:30, I should leave my home by **2:35.**

33. The speed at which the plane flew from Dayton to St. Louis is the distance of 334 miles divided by the time traveled, which was 1.5 hours (accounting for the change in time zone). This yields approximately **222.67 miles per hour.** Similarly, we can divide the St. Louis–Pittsburgh distance of 562 miles by 2 hours to obtain **281 miles per hour.**

34. (a) **6.97 + 1.99 + 1.19 + 2x = 40.53**

(b) The equation in Part (a) simplifies to $2x + 10.15 = 40.53$, which is equivalent to $2x = 30.38$. Therefore, $x = 15.19$: each gallon of paint costs **$15.19.**

35. The area of the driveway is the area of the large semicircle (radius 27 feet) minus the area of the lawn (radius 12 feet): $\frac{1}{2}\pi(27)^2 - \frac{1}{2}\pi(12)^2$, or approximately 918.92 square feet. Dividing by 9 converts this area to square yards, yielding 102.10 square yards (1 square yard equals 9 square feet). To find volume, multiply area by height. The "height" is the depth of 6 inches, which equals $\frac{1}{6}$ of a yard, so the job requires **17.02 cubic yards** of material.

36. To find the area of the field, we must know the length of the base of the large triangle. To find the length, multiply both sides of the ratio equation $\frac{18}{15} = \frac{B}{900}$ by 900, and then simplify to get $B = 1080$. Therefore, the area of the field is $\frac{1}{2}(1080)(900)$, or **486,000 square feet.**

37. The balance is $500 - (14 \times 30) + (2 \times 712) - 65$, or **$1439.**

38. The bottom and top of the tank each have an area of $\pi(15)^2$, or 225π square feet, since the radius of the tank is 15 feet. The tank's side has an area of 600π square feet (found by multiplying the circumference of 30π by the height of 20). Therefore, the total surface area of the tank is $(600 + 450)\pi$ square feet, or approximately 3297 square feet (using 3.14 for π). Each gallon of paint covers about 250 square feet, so the town will need approximately 13.19 gallons of paint. Since only whole gallons of paint are sold, the town must buy **14 gallons.**

39. Each cylindrical tank has a volume of $\pi r^2 h$, where $r = 16$ feet and $h = 85$ feet. So each tank will hold $21,760\pi$ cubic feet of oil. Using 3.14 for π, this equals approximately 68,326.4 cubic feet of oil. Therefore, you will need $1,000,000 \div 68,326.4 \approx 14.636$, or **15 tanks.**

40. (a) The table below shows the offense's position at the beginning and end of each play, as well as the resulting down number.

Play Number	Beginning Yard Line	Yards Gained	Ending Yard Line	Resulting Down Number
1	20 (own)	6	20 + 6 = 26	2
2	26	−2	26 + (−2) = 24	3
3	24	9	24 + 9 = 33	1
4	33	8	33 + 8 = 41	2
5	41	−9	41 + (−9) = 32	3
6	32	18	32 + 18 = 50	1
7	50	12	50 − 12 = 38	1
8	38 (opponent's)	Interception		

As this table shows, our team earned **three first downs:** at the end of Plays 3, 6, and 7.

(b) As the table above shows, the offense had advanced to the **opponent's 38 yard line** before Play 8 took place.

41. (a) **1.86 × 10⁵ miles per second**

(b) Multiply 365 by 24 (to convert from days to hours), then multiply by 60 (to convert from hours to minutes), and then multiply again by 60 (to convert from minutes to seconds). This is $(365)(24)(60)^2$, which yields 31,536,000, or **3.1536 × 10⁷ seconds** in one year.

(c) Multiply 1.86×10^5 by 3.1536×10^7 to obtain approximately **5.866 × 10¹² miles per year.**

(d) As determined in Part (c), the speed of light is 5.866×10^{12} miles per year. Multiply this by 4.2 (the distance in light-years to the star) to get **2.464 × 10¹³ miles.**

42. (a) We simply divide 207 by 176 to obtain 1.1761 (approximately). So $207 is **117.61%** of $176.

(b) The amount of increase from $176 to $207 is $117.61\% - 100\% = $ **17.61%.**

(c) The amount you owe per month is $207 − $176 = $31. For the year you will owe $31 × 12 = **$372.**

43. (a) Since $6.00 ÷ 5.75 = 1.0435$ (approximately), the first percentage increase was **4.35%.** The other two increases were **6.67%** (from $6.00 to $6.40) and **9.38%** (from $6.40 to $7.00).

(b) The increase from $5.75 to $7.00 is **21.74%.**

(c) **No,** the sum of the three percentages in Part (a) is 20.40%, which is not the percentage found in Part (b). This is not a problem. The three smaller percentages do not sum to the larger percentage, but they are related by multiplication. That is, if we take into account some rounding error, we see that $(1.0435)(1.0667)(1.0938) \approx 1.2174$.

44. (a) The cost of using concrete is $(17.02)(75.40)$, or **$1283.31.** To determine the cost using asphalt, first calculate the number of tons of asphalt in 17.02 cubic yards. Since each cubic yard weighs 1.5 tons, $(17.02)(1.5) = 25.53$ tons of asphalt would be needed. At $29.70 per ton, asphalt would cost $(25.53)($29.70$)$, or **$758.24.**

(b) The **asphalt** is less expensive, by **$525.07.**

45. (a)

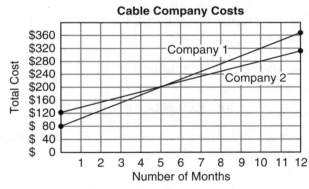

(b) The cost is the same where the two lines intersect. This occurs **after 5 months.**

(c) At $x = 3$, the line for **Company 1** is lower, so it is the better deal.

(d) When $x \geq 8$, the line for **Company 2** is lower, so it is the better deal.

46. For Beau's Bikes, the algebraic sentence is $y = 10t$. For Celine's Cycles, it is $y = 4t + 15$.

47. (a) Since $10^2 = 100$ and $11^2 = 121$, $\sqrt{106}$ must be **between 10 and 11 yards.**

(b) Since the length is between 30 and 33 feet (10 and 11 yards converted to feet), the city should purchase **3 pieces of wood.**

(c) Three pieces of wood is 36 feet, so there will be **between 3 and 6 feet of wood unused.**

48. (a) Solve the equation $10t = 4t + 15$ for t. The cost is the same at $t =$ **2.5 hours.**

    (b) The cost of renting a bike from Beau for two hours is $20, while the cost of renting a bike from Celine for two hours is $15 + (2)(4)$, or $23. So the couple should rent from **Beau's Bikes.**

49. (a) The ingredients for each pizza will cost $75¢ + 40¢ + 60¢ = 175¢$, or **$1.75.**

    (b) Your friends donated a total of $20. Dividing this by $1.75 yields approximately 11.43, so you can make **11 whole pizzas.**

    (c) With your added dollar you have $21. Dividing this by $1.75 yields exactly 12, so you can make **12 whole pizzas.**

50. (a) The total cost for each bucket of popcorn is $5¢ + 2¢ + 25¢$ or $32¢$. Since each bucket of popcorn sells for $300¢$, the profit per bucket is $300¢ - 32¢ = 268¢$, or $2.68. When this is multiplied by 115 buckets, the profit is **$308.20.**

    (b) Solve the equation $115(c - 32) = 36,570$ for c, where c is the amount you charge for each bucket of popcorn. This equation simplifies to $c - 32 = 318$, so $c = 350$. That means you should charge $350¢$, or **$3.50 per bucket.**

51. (a) First notice that $5 + 2 + 1 = 8$. Then note that $1216 \div 8 = 152$. So the three players scored $(152)(5)$, $(152)(2)$, and $(152)(1)$ points. This is **760, 304,** and **152 points.**

    (b) The third-highest scorer's total is $\frac{1}{5}$, or **20%,** of the total of the highest scorer.

52. The earth's radius is half the diameter of 1.275×10^7 meters, which is 6.375×10^6 meters. So the volume of the earth is $\frac{4}{3}\pi(6.375 \times 10^6)^3$, or approximately **$1.085 \times 10^{21}$ cubic meters.**

53. (a) This triangle is an **isosceles right triangle.**

    (b) $180° - 90° - 39° =$ **51°.**

    (c) The sum of the angle the two stabilizing wires make with each other and the angles that they each make with the ground is $180°$. Thus, that angle is $180° - 45° - 51° = 84°$. It is an **acute triangle, and one of its angles measures 84°.** (Some students may also determine that the triangle is scalene.)

54. Of the 200 boys, we expect $23\frac{1}{2}\%$ to attend college within 175 miles of our school. This is $(200)(0.235)$, or 47. Similarly, we expect $(150)(0.1966667)$, or 29.5 girls, to do the same. Rounding up, we expect **77 of our students** to attend college within 175 miles of our school.

55. (a) When interest is added at the end of each quarter, the amount in the bank becomes 1.01 times what it was previously. At the end of the first quarter, this is 1000×1.01, or $1010. At the end of the second quarter, the account is worth 1010×1.01, or $1020.10. Repeat this calculation eight times to find the account balance after two years, which is approximately **$1082.86.**

    (b) **This savings plan is not enough.**

56. The sale price for each pair of clogs is $33.99(\frac{2}{3})$, which is $22.66. The sale price for each shirt is $18.00(\frac{3}{5})$, which is $10.80. Since Stephanie plans to buy two pairs of clogs and three shirts, the total cost will be $22.66(2) + 10.80(3)$, or $77.72. So **Stephanie does not have enough money to pay in cash.** She still needs **$7.72** to buy all five items.

57. (a) Using B for boy and G for girl, the Li family could have any one of the following 16 possibilities: **BBBB, BBBG, BBGB, BGBB, GBBB, BBGG, BGBG, BGGB, GBBG, GBGB, GGBB, GGGB, GGBG, GBGG, BGGG, GGGG.**

  (b) The probability that the family has exactly two boys and two girls in some order is $\frac{6}{16}$, or $\frac{3}{8}$.

58. (a) The probability of picking a green jelly bean is $\frac{10}{100}$. Once this green jelly bean has been picked and kept, 99 jelly beans remain in the bag, of which 20 are red. So the probability of picking a red jelly bean under these circumstances is $\frac{20}{99}$. Multiplying these two probabilities and simplifying yields the final answer, which is $\frac{2}{99}$.

  (b) The probability of picking the first orange jelly bean is $\frac{10}{100}$. Then only 9 orange jelly beans remain in a bag of 99. So the probability of picking a second orange jelly bean is $\frac{9}{99}$. Multiplying these two probabilities and simplifying yields a probability of $\frac{1}{110}$.

59. (a) The length of $\overline{YW}$ is $(YW)^2 + 100^2 = 260^2$. This simplifies to $(YW)^2 = 57{,}600$, or **$YW = 240$ yards.** Once this is determined, we can see that $ZW = 360$. The hypotenuse XZ of the larger triangle is the square root of $100^2 + 360^2$, which is $\sqrt{139{,}600}$ yards. The length of $\overline{XZ}$ is approximately **373.63 yards.**

  (b) The fence costs $8 per linear foot, which is $24 per linear yard. The perimeter of the outer triangle measures $373.63 + 100 + 360$, or 833.63 yards. Therefore, the cost will be $(24)(833.63)$ or **$20,007.12.**

60. (a) The area of each triangular face of the pyramid is $\frac{1}{2}(50)(28)$, or 700 square feet. Since there are four such faces, the total number of square feet that needs to be shingled is **2800 square feet.**

  (b) Each bundle of shingles will cover 1.5×20, or 30 square feet, so $93\frac{1}{3}$ bundles of shingles will be needed (found by dividing 2800 by 30). Since fractional bundles of shingles are not sold, we will have to buy **94 bundles.**